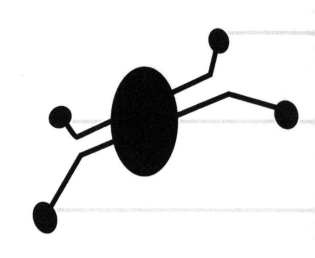

Current and Future
Codey-B Books by R.A. Güembes

CODEY  B

by R.A. Güembes

JOURNAL_ENTRY_001

> Why "Self" Care?

To improve thyself and to create a happy,
beautiful, caring, giving, joyful,
wonderful world._

"Haaaaaaaaaapy!!!"

Bring Codey-B to life! Scan this code with your smart device throughout the book.

Launch the Intro.

> Use a QR reader application or use your built-in camera feature using any new equipment.

CODEY-B VOCABULARY

Before you begin the story, learn Codey-B's world through his words.

Abundance: Plentifulness of the good things of life; prosperity.

Alertness: The state of being ready to see, understand, and act in a particular situation.

Affirmation: Something declared to be true; a positive statement or judgment.

Art: The conscious use of the imagination in the production of objects intended to be contemplated or appreciated as beautiful, as in the arrangement of forms, sounds, or words.

Awareness: Conscious knowledge.

Boundaries: Something that indicates a border or limit.

Coding: Instructions for a computer (as within a piece of software).

Confident: Having a feeling or belief that you can do something well or succeed at something : having confidence.

Environmentalist: One concerned about environmental quality especially of the human environment with respect to the control of pollution

Gratitude: A feeling of appreciation or thanks.

Happiness: The state of being happy : Joy.

Inspiration: The excitement of the mind or emotions to a high level of feeling or activity.

Imagination: The ability to form mental images of things that are not present to the senses or not considered to be real.

Kindness: An instance of kind behavior.

Leadership: Capacity or ability to lead.

Lovingness: A loving manner; affectionate bearing or conduct.

Mental Health: A state of emotional and psychological well-being in which an individual is able to use his or her cognitive and emotional capabilities, function in society, and meet the ordinary demands of everyday life.

Mindfulness: The state or quality of being mindful; attention; needfulness; intention; purpose.

Mindset: A fixed state of mind.

Nutrition: The act or process of nourishing or being nourished.

Recycle: Convert (waste) into reusable material.

Self Care: Care for oneself

Sustainable: Able to be maintained at a certain rate or level.

Yoga: A system of stretching and positional exercises derived from this discipline to promote good health, fitness, and control of the mind.

CODEY B

WORKBOOK+JOURNAL

> TABLE_OF_CONTENTS

_PROLOGUE

PRESENT DAY

> Starship Login

Time to build a positive mindset,
write down life goals, and participate.

Let's change the world together!

-CB

_About_Me

> **KNOW THYSELF.** What are your goals for the future?
Who are you now? Visualize who you want to be.
Write it down and draw it.

> **Who do I want to be?**

Write it:

Draw a happy you.

> Who do you envision yourself to be?

Write it:

Draw yourself.

_My_Superpower

> **CHECK THE BOXES** below and/or write in your own superpower.

- ☐ I can do anything
- ☐ I love coding
- ☐ I like to build things
- ☐ I care for the environment
- ☐ I love animals
- ☐ My care for the planet
- ☐ Natural leader
- ☐ My kindness
- ☐ My imagination
- ☐ My powerful brain
- ☐ I make cool things
- ☐ I never give up
- ☐ My funny jokes
- ☐ I am a good friend
- ☐ I help others
- ☐ My great ideas
- ☐ I love to dance
- ☐ _____
- ☐ _____
- ☐ _____

Great job! Pick one and work on it more.

Draw yourself as a Superhero!

Name it:

_____

_Your_Mind
_Your_Life

> YOU MATTER!

Self-Care Tips

- **LIVE HEALTHY,** eat healthy foods, get enough sleep, and exercise regularly.
- **PRACTICE GOOD HYGIENE.** Good hygiene is important for social, medical, and psychological reasons in that it not only reduces the risk of illness, but it also improves the way others view you and how you view yourself.
- **SEE FRIENDS** to build your sense of belonging. Consider joining a support group to make new friends.
- **TRY TO DO SOMETHING YOU ENJOY** every day. That might mean dancing, watching a favorite TV show, working in the garden, painting or reading.
- **FIND WAYS TO RELAX,** like meditation, yoga, taking a bath, playing games and/or taking a walk in nature.
- **LEARN FINANCES AND ABUNDANCE.** It's important to think big and know how to save and invest your money. Build your perfect life, invest in yourself.
- **JOURNAL** your wins and goals, daily.

_Working_Toward_Goals

> **BE CLEAR.** Set goals and watch your life become different once your goals are achieved. Always congratulate yourself for achieving your goals. Even small ones. It's a sign of accomplishment!

Goal Tips

1. **Focus on your strengths.**
2. **Focus on solving problems.**
3. **Focus on the future instead of reviewing hurts from the past.**
4. **Focus on your life instead of your illness.**

> **Write Six Goals for Yourself.**

1.

2.

3.

4.

5.

6.

_Affirmations

> **DAILY AFFIRMATIONS** are simply positive
statements you tell yourself every day.
This small investment in positive thinking can
have a big impact on one's well-being, and it's
especially beneficial to build your self-image
and learn how to navigate your feelings.
Here are a few to get you started.

1. I have many talents.
2. I don't have to be perfect to be worthy.
3. Making mistakes helps me grow.
4. I am good at solving problems.
5. I'm not afraid of a challenge.
6. I am smart.
7. I am capable.
8. I am a good friend.
9. I am loved for who I am.
10. I remember that bad feelings come and go.
11. I'm proud of myself.
12. I have a great personality.
13. I am enough.
14. My thoughts and feelings are important.
15. I'm unique and special.
16. I can be assertive without being aggressive.
17. I can stand up for what I believe in.
18. I know right from wrong.

> **Write Nine Affirmations for Yourself.**

1. _____

2. _____

3. _____

4. _____

5. _____

6. _____

7. _____

8. _____

9. _____

_My_First_Line_Of_Code

> **CODEY-B** learned his first line of Python Code from his father, it changed him forever. He now writes code for his friendly bots and is healing the world one code at a time.

From Codey-B and the Python's Code: Book One

"It's like Magic. First, you create your algorithm, which is setting up the rules for your code. Then you write your code."

"Finally, you end up with code that could do very magical things. You can program computers by writing software to do many things. I like to teach my A.I. Robots my personality to tailor them as my 'A.I. Friends'. They become your loyal companion and know what you like!"

"It's like poetry," he would say.

"That is how I learned how to write my first line of code. Learning my first variable."

"First, we have to make your name a *variable*."

"A variable?"

"A *variable* is like a box that holds numbers, words, or even tiny bits of code! When the code runs, it opens the box and uses it. Look at this."

> myName = " "

myName is a *variable*. Now write your name in between the quotations.

> myName = "   "

"Okay, now let's run this code with the rest of it."

Python Code: *myname = "Codey-B"*
        print("Hello there, ",myName,"!
                Let's play a fun game!")

That was my introduction to code, Python code.

"Make code fun and functional!"

_How_To_Turn Earth's_Challenges Into_Wins

> **BE THE NEXT TECH ENVIRONMENTALIST** (Eco-Scientist)!
The world needs you! How would you fix it?

1. Draw the type of pollution you see
in the world.

2. Draw how you would fix it.

> Draw a robot and you fixing pollution.

Name it:

_Interview_Someone

> **RESEARCH** and interview people around you to gather your own data.

> **BECOMING AN EARTH SCIENTIST** takes courage and imagination. You are speaking up for causes that you believe in and that benefit from you taking a stand. Here are some starter questions to start asking yourself and others on interviews.

1. What is the most interesting or useful conversation to have?

2. What's going on in the world? And What are the facts?

3. What do we do about all the division?

4. How do we get people on the same page?

5. What do we do about the planet?

6. What is the best way to live?

7. What do I do about my anger?

8. What should I do with my life?

9. What action should I take in the world?

10. What are my obligations to my fellow human beings?

11. How should I handle the success or power that I hold?

> Draw yourself interviewing someone.

_Question_Everything

> **BE CURIOUS** about the world? And how it works.
Codey-B is always asking himself the same questions.
Try out his formula for problem solving.

Write Down Any Question. (Q1):

Write the Answer to (Q1). (A1):

Question Two (Q2):
(Ask in response to (A1).)

_____

_____

_____

Answer Two (A2):
(Final answer.)

_____

_____

_____

Example:
(Q1) Are roses blue?
(A1) Sometimes.
(Q2) When?
(A2) When they come into bloom
at the beginning of summer from
a genetically modified seed.

_Volunteer

> **GET ACTIVE AND GET INVOLVED!** There are many
organizations looking for volunteers. Find one
that best aligns with you and volunteer!
Giving is creating abundance around you.

Ideas on how you can help[1]:

1. Volunteer at a local animal shelter.
2. Gather information about volunteering at a
   local nature center, farm, or zoo.
3. Donate newspapers, dog beds, or other pet
   supplies to a local animal shelter.
4. Place bird feeders in the yard for
   local wild birds.
5. Offer to walk a neighbor's dog.
6. Pet sit for a neighbor when they go out of town.
7. Keep food or water out for stray animals and
   contact a local animal shelter to take them in.
8. Foster a pet in your home.
9. Help a local pet rescue group at an
   adoption event.
10. Adopt a pet!
11. Walk around the neighborhood with a garbage bag
    and pick up trash on the side of the road.
12. Offer to rake leaves, pick up sticks, or mow
    the lawn of a neighbor.
13. Plant flowers for a neighbor or in a communal
    neighborhood area.
14. Start a community garden.
15. Collect and deliver supplies to neighbors
    who have just had a baby, undergone surgery,
    or experienced a house fire.
16. Collect money for new playground equipment
    or another neighborhood need.

17. Volunteering can be as simple as making people smile. Draw pictures or write notes to deliver to your neighbors.
18. Make it seasonal. In the fall, offer to rake leaves. In the winter, be available to help shovel snow.
19. Coordinate a collection of used books in your neighborhood and donate them to your local school.
20. Coordinate a neighborhood garage sale and donate the proceeds to a local charity.
21. Cook or serve meals at a homeless shelter.
22. Make care packages for the homeless. Include travel-sized toiletries, granola bars, and bottled water. Carry them with you in the car to hand out when you have the opportunity.
23. Donate books or art supplies to a homeless shelter for children.
24. Collect coats and give to a homeless shelter in winter.
25. Sponsor a child through Toys for Tots or the Angel Tree to make sure these children have magical holidays.
26. Check with your local soup kitchen to see if young children can assist with setting tables or handing out small fruits like apples and bananas.
27. Shop for a toy to give away, and then have your child give it to a child in need.
28. Gather canned foods to deposit at a local food bank.
29. Have your child sort through old toys they don't play with anymore and donate them to Goodwill or another local charity group.
30. Participate in local events, such as 5Ks, fun runs, or other events that donate proceeds to local charities helping those in need.

_Teamwork_at_Code-Base

> **A PLAN OF ACTION** can make your
dreams come true. Code-Base is run
like a business. The Eco-Bots™
create value for people by cleaning
polluted places, generating abundance
in the form of a clean life and
money. Then we reinvest it back into
our business.

Learn how to make money, $$ learn how
to save it, $$ and learn how to
invest it $$ by living in abundance
and being the happiest you!

Be mindful, learn and study finances.
Invest in you.

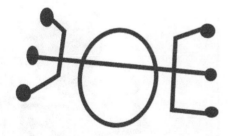

_Let's_Do_This!

> There's a lot to be done.

\$tart

> Get me home!\$\$\$\$\$

_Journal_Tips

> **Write in your Journal often.**

1. Write down your dreams.
2. Write down your goals.
3. Write down your achievements,
4. Write down what you are grateful for!

LET'S GO!

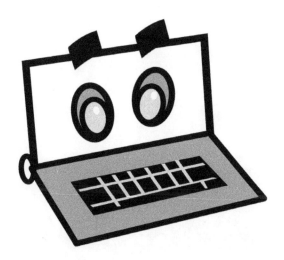

_Journal_Entry_001

DATE / /

_Journal_Entry_002

_Journal_Entry_003

_Journal_Entry_002

_Journal_Entry_003

_Journal_Entry_004

_Journal_Entry_005

_Journal_Entry_007

DATE
/   /

DATE   /   /

_Journal_Entry_009

/   /

_Journal_Entry_010

_Journal_Entry_011

_Journal_Entry_012

_Journal_Entry_013

_Journal_Entry_014

_Journal_Entry_015

_Journal_Entry_014

_Journal_Entry_015

_Journal_Entry_016

_Journal_Entry_017

DATE
/   /

_Journal_Entry_018

_Journal_Entry_019

_Journal_Entry_020

_Congratulations, you did it! Be sure to share and play the Game on Roblox.

SCAN ME

Play the Codey-B game
to win special prizes.

RESOURCES

1. **Mental Health America**
   www.mhanational.org

2. **Be Strong**
   Mentally Strong, Resilient,
   Free of Bullying and Hopeful.
   www.bestrong.global

3. **Get Involved**
   www.codeybworld.com

www.ingramcontent.com/pod-product-compliance
Lightning Source LLC
Chambersburg PA
CBHW051115050326
40690CB00006B/796